Dealing with Grief

How to Cope and Heal After the Death of a Loved One

by Paul Stanton

Table of Contents

Introduction

Having to deal with the loss of someone or something you care very deeply about can have you in for some very painful times. Whether you lost a dear friend, family member, pet, or even something like a self-defining career or a long-term relationship, the sadness and pain you feel is a normal part of the grieving process. It's important for you to understand that the emotions you're feeling are your mind, body and soul's natural way of responding to and dealing with a significant loss. When someone you love dies, or you lose something you love, a very significant part of your life is suddenly removed, and your body and mind will react with what seems to be a painful flood of emotions as a way to try and adapt to the sudden change to the best of its ability. The pain typically manifests in a number of different ways, but you're likely to go through an experience that includes a wide range of very difficult emotions, and it may even seem as though the hurt just won't let up and that the deep wound may never heal. And although you may feel like you have no control over your emotions and mental state at this time, it's important to remember that this kind of a reaction is somewhat normal, and it's also something that you can start to gain control over using appropriate methods.

1

Believe it or not, after a great loss, the grieving experience is actually the first step to healing. Different people handle significant loss in different ways, but it's important to understand that the way in which you handle the grieving process actually influences your overall emotional and physical well-being. The pain associated with the loss of a loved one should never be allowed to diminish the overall quality of your life — at least not on a permanent basis. This very important consideration shines a light upon two categories into which the effects of a significant loss are classified: healthy and unhealthy ways of grieving. A healthy way of coping with loss allows you to proceed through the stages of grief and come out of the entire experience feeling refreshed, renewed, and ready to move on with your life. Unhealthy ways of dealing with loss are indicative of a process through which grief comes with numerous complications that make it nearly impossible for you to let go of the pain you feel, leaving it buried deep inside like a dormant volcano ready to erupt again at any time. As a result, permanent damage and trauma may be inflicted on other areas in your life, hence affecting your quality of life, and even your ability to make healthy decisions.

In your current state of emotions, the very confusing rollercoaster of feelings you're experiencing might become so extreme at times that you lose clarity and can't even think straight. This is when guidance and structured insight into the proper grieving process will come in handy, arming you with an important set of skills that will help you heal and move on with your life, and setting you well on your way to recovery. This book was written to help you better understand the grieving process and to help you become fully equipped to deal with your grief in a healthy, constructive way.

Chapter 1: The Stages of Grief, Symptoms, and Myths

Grief isn't just associated with a loved one's death, although it is indeed understandable that the death of a loved one is generally considered as the ultimate grief-trigger. There are many more sources of grief, including some seemingly unrelated events like your health suffering, losing your long-running financial freedom or stability, breaking off from a long-term or very promising relationship (breakup/divorce), having to retire, moving house or selling the only house you've ever known as your home, compromised security and suddenly having to fear for your safety, or even getting hit by the reality that you have to give up your life-long dream.

Some of the more commonly acknowledged causes of grief go back to the death of a loved one, the death of a pet (or having to give up your pet), a loved one having to deal with a serious illness, a miscarriage or even a strained relationship between you and a good friend or family member. The significance of the loss is unique to you as an individual, governed by the extent to which you had an emotional attachment to the person or object of your loss.

What's important is that you understand it's only natural for you to feel as if your emotions are playing tricks on you and that the pain you feel isn't anything unusual. Looking at it from a more psychiatric point of view, Swiss-American psychiatrist Elisabeth Kübler-Ross (8 July, 1926–24 August, 2004), who broke new ground in her pioneering near-death field of study, famously popularized her five-stage theory of the grieving process. Basically there are five stages you'll have to go through in order to deal with your grief, starting with denial, then anger, and next bargaining, followed by depression, and finally acceptance.

Now, it's in no way necessary at all to try to memorize the Kubler-Ross model of assessing the stages of grief because that won't really help you much in actually coping and dealing with your loss. For now though, what you should do is at least try to identify which stage of grief you're currently on. There is absolutely no time limit suggested or imposed for each stage you go through, but what's important is that you get through these stages, ideally in your own time and in your own way. Progressively working through the five Kubler-Ross stages of grief is generally indicative of a healthy way of coping with your loss, while getting permanently stuck on one of these stages (typically the depression stage) is a sign of an unhealthy way of dealing with your loss, during which time grieving complications come into play. The ways of dealing with such grieving complications and effectively finding a way to break out of the grieving stage you're stuck in will be discussed in Chapter 4; but for now, learning to identify which stage of grief you're currently on will do you a world of good.

Denial

This stage of the grieving process usually passes by rather quickly and can often exist for mere seconds and minutes after you learn about your loss. Grievers typically experience this stage of grief in a variety of different ways, from flat out refusing to believe the news of their loss and choosing not to take it on board, right down to briefly experiencing feelings of sheer shock, which are then followed by the advancement to the next stage of grief. Basically you either cannot believe that your loss has indeed befallen you, or you simply refuse to accept your loss.

Anger

This stage of the grieving process is characterized by denial giving way to the reality of your loss sinking in, causing you to question the fairness of the situation. You'll ask yourself questions why exactly this is happening to you, what have you done to deserve something like this and you might even want to find someone or something to blame. Questioning one's faith is another way through which this stage of the grieving process manifests, and you generally feel enraged—you have come to terms with the news of your loss, but you haven't quite accepted it fully. A part of you feels as if someone or something needs to be punished, and after that, everything will go back to normal and perhaps everybody else will realize that "there's no loss".

Bargaining

This stage of the grieving process is usually characterized by opening up communication channels with a deity or higher power. Even in the event that you may not exactly be the most religious person, you'll find yourself trying to cut a deal with someone or something you perceive to be of a higher power (like a god you worship, life in general or something like "Karma"). What you'd typically propose to exchange is the reversal of your loss (or your loss simply turning out not to be true) for better conduct on your part. It could be very specific or general, like you might have perhaps recently done something you're not very proud of, or you promise to reform your life in some way and become a "better person" all-round. Basically in this stage of the grieving process, you try to look for a compromise in exchange for the reversal or nullification of your loss.

Depression

All three previous stages of grief discussed are usually accompanied by a range of reactions, a very common one is crying (weeping). Crying is almost an inevitable part of this particular stage of the grieving process (depression), but your depression can be expressed in a number of other ways. A very common manifestation of this depression is characterized by feelings of being "all cried out," when you simply feel as if your tears have dried up because you just cannot cry any more. What normally happens then is the sadness of your life engulfing you to the point where the quality of your life suffers in some way. You either feel as if there is a void which simply cannot be filled, or in extreme cases, you don't even want to go on with your life. You feel as if there is no point to your life if you are without whomever or whatever you've lost. You may even start to question the meaning of life, your faith or wonder about your own purpose in life (and whether it's even worth fulfilling). At this stage, grief can get particularly difficult to deal with, especially since there is no set time limit for you to have to move on from this stage, so you'll naturally deal with your grief in your own unique way. If your altered state of existence directly threatens the long-term quality of your life with permanent damage, that's when this stage of the grieving process becomes unhealthy and that's when you need to pay close attention to what to do when the grieving process develops complications (as discussed in Chapter 4).

It's otherwise a healthy part of the process to feel depressed—the important thing is not to allow your depression to inflict permanent alterations on the quality of your life.

Acceptance

When you finally make peace with the reality of your loss, the healing process becomes much easier. This stage of the grieving process is characterized by your acknowledgment of the loss you suffered, and more importantly, your realization that life simply has to go on. You're not letting go in the sense that you're actively trying to forget your loss or replace who or what you've lost, but you're rather coming to terms with the fact that it did indeed happen and you just have to carry on with life. You typically know you've accepted your loss if you notice a range of things going back to normal, no matter how big or small they may be, such as smiling again or rediscovering your temporarily lost ability to laugh.

Keep in mind that while experiencing any or all of the stages of the grieving process forms a natural part of the healing process, you may not explicitly experience all of these stages. You also don't have to experience each stage in any order, for any standard period of time, or with any standard degree of intensity. The ability to identify which stage you're on is only significant to your coping and healing ability if you can distinguish some changes. You have to look for differences and progression in the way you grieve because that is how you cope and work your way towards healing.

Grief Symptoms

As far as the symptoms of grief go, these pretty much encompass the reactionary emotions you feel following a loss. Not everything you feel or do in the wake of a loss is a direct symptom of grief, but the most common symptoms include a very painful sadness, disbelief, shock, or anger. You might also feel guilty (with or without justifiable reason) or scared. In some cases, grief induces some physical symptoms, such as deteriorating health, a weakened immune system, weight gain or loss, nausea, muscle pains or having to endure sleeping disorders. Again, these are not meant to be explicitly defined symptoms that constitute the entire range of what you'll go through as part of the grieving process. They're only common symptoms, each of which affects each individual differently.

Common Myths about Grief

While these beliefs we'll explore could otherwise be very easily dismissed as myths with a bit of common sense, when you find yourself having to deal with a significant loss, common sense often goes out of the window. The grieving heart (and mind) can play some nasty emotional tricks on you and you may find yourself more susceptible to belief systems that are otherwise not in line with your usual logical and critical thinking.

One of the most common myths associated with grief is that the ultimate goal is to "get over your loss." In reality, you will never really fully get over the loss of someone or something which was a significant part of your life, so the aim is to cope with it and continue living your life having made peace with the fact that they're longer part of your life instead. You're not trying to forget who you've lost, but you're rather working to live with the pain and experience the pain in a way that impacts less and less on your quality of life.

Another common myth about the grieving process is that people in your life will help you avoid experiencing the pain of grieving through their avoidance of talking about your loss or triggering memories of whom you've lost. Dealing with your loss by confronting reality head-on is one of the fastest ways through which to heal, even though it may be very hard to cope with in the moment.

The myth about how long grief should last is also a very common one, largely due to its confusion with cultural mourning periods of a loved one, particularly a spouse. The myth goes that you shouldn't grieve for more than 1-2 years maximum, but that's exactly what it is—a myth. The only right time frame within which you should grieve is one that is dictated by how you feel. You're obviously not going to wake up every single morning for the rest of your life in tears, but depending on how significant your loss was, in one way or another you actually never stop grieving. What happens is that you learn to deal with the loss in a way that doesn't hit you as hard as it used to, with the passage of time. You'll stop visibly grieving when you do—simple as that. So don't put a deadline on your healing process.

If you are adequately armed with some useful knowledge about the workings of the grieving process, you'll be better prepared to cope with your loss more effectively as you go along on your path to healing.

Chapter 2: Finding Your Own Way to Deal with Grief

It cannot be emphasized enough that everybody has a different way of dealing with a loss and the grief that follows. That's why it's important for you to find your own way of grieving, *falling* into your own way of grieving to a certain extent. Be careful not to fall into clinical depression though, because that's when grief becomes unhealthy.

This tailored way of coping with your grief entails giving in to the pain and sadness. You simply have to allow yourself to cry or express your anger in whichever way feels natural. Let it out and don't try to stifle your natural reaction as it forms in response to your loss. Don't let it get out of control though—yes you're hurting and nobody (including you) should expect anything else of you, but dealing with your loss should never be used as an excuse to throw away control of your life. Be careful about what you say and whom you say it to. Be honest about your feelings but don't assume that the daily challenges and stresses of life are going to let up to let you go through your grieving process with a pat on the back. What you'll realize is that the pain and sadness of your loss pretty much engulfs every other daily struggle. It may seem as if there is only one problem to deal with it, which is managing your grief.

So, in dealing with your grief by embracing your own unique way of coping with your loss, do what comes naturally and spontaneously. Allow your reaction to take place and let it out. If for example a loved one has passed away, it's only natural for you to want to cry. Cry. Don't try to stifle it. This is not the time to be "strong." Being strong won't help anybody. This is particularly true in the case of collective grief, when perhaps there is a child involved. If you've split up with a spouse for example, or perhaps a spouse has passed-on, a child who is at the center of the grief also goes through the five stages of grief. The effects of one of those stages could compound the process further, during which time the child feels angry about the loss you've both suffered. If you stifle your grief as part of your attempt to be "strong," the child's anger and blame may be directed at you because you might quite easily be perceived not to be experiencing the effects of loss. Embrace the natural reactions that come to you; if the people around you are aware of your loss and if they're aware that it is having a significant impact on you, they'll subsequently offer their help in more ways than they usually do.

Simply put—don't try to play any role society may have for you. Grieve how you want to grieve by giving in to what comes naturally.

Chapter 3: Taking Control of Your Grieving Process

Following on from the previous chapter, which emphasized the need to grieve in your own unique way, while you're in a sense falling into your own way of grieving; it still has to be a controlled fall. If you don't take control of the effects of your grieving process, you run the risk of falling into depression and that can make for some challenging complications to get through.

Yes, you're allowed to be sad, and you're allowed to feel as if the whole world is against you, but this doesn't mean your entire life should come to a standstill. The world definitely keeps turning and if you stop doing your bit for too long, life can very quickly leave you behind. You don't want to have to find a way of coping with your loss and then have that challenge compounded by a reality of magnified responsibilities to have to get back to as a result of you letting yourself go too much.

When you are going through the grieving process, it has never been more important to take good care of yourself. Pay attention to your body's daily needs, like personal hygiene (don't skip baths or meals more than you usually do) and make it a point to take care of your physical health. Instead of letting your grief-induced reactions serve as a destructive force, channel that negative energy and re-direct it into something constructive. If you're suffering from insomnia and can't sleep for example, find a way to invest that energy into something productive or creative. This is an important part of coping with the new reality you've been left with as a result of your loss. If a loved one died for example, try to think about what they would have wanted you to do in the situation you're in right now. Would they want you to sit around and go over everything, over and over again until you go insane, or would they want you to maybe go to work so that you can financially support yourself?

However, with that said, don't try to force things—again, just do what comes naturally but don't linger too long in a state where you're stuck in limbo. Don't let your loss induce oblivion. Take care of yourself so that you only have the loss itself to contend with. Remember not to try and stifle your feelings either—you can shed a tear while you're taking a bath, but continue to live your life.

Maintaining a measure of control over your grief in this way puts the power in your hands and allows you to heal quicker. Remember that you're not trying to forget whom or what you've lost, rather you're training yourself to enter a new state of mind in which the pain you'll carry forever becomes more and more bearable.

Another way through which to take control of your grieving process is to solicit support. This is the only time when your efforts to deal with your loss should be dictated by something which goes against what comes naturally to you. Under no circumstances should you go through a prolonged period of your grieving process in complete isolation. Do not grieve alone. There are definitely some times when you'll feel as if you only want to be by yourself, but don't extend periods of isolation. You will be much better served dealing with your grief in the midst of your friends and family, or at least one other person who either shares your grief or empathizes with you. Join a support group featuring other grievers who have experienced a similar loss to yours if you have to, or even talk to a counselor or therapist. You can reach out to somebody online if that's your only viable medium of communicating with others, but don't try to grieve in isolation.

Sharing your grief is very important because it draws on one of the most powerful features of what makes human beings successful as a species—the ability to come together and effectively halve a problem by sharing it. It might not feel like it makes any difference in the moment, but sharing your grief by dealing with your loss in the midst of others will go a long way in speeding up the healing process. The people you surround yourself with will help you maintain control of other areas of your life while you try and cope with the immediate grief.

Chapter 4: What to Do When the Negative Effects Won't Go Away

While it's normal (and expected) for you to experience intense feelings of numbing and saddening pain following a loss, such emotions naturally become more bearable with the passage of time. You don't get over your loss or forget about it, but rather learn to live with the associated pain to such an extent that it no longer harasses you as intensely as it did before.

Sometimes grief can get quite complicated though, particularly if you're dealing with unprecedented levels of trauma or if the loss you've suffered is just too devastating to handle. Grief complications can be particularly hard to deal with because often if you're the one who's suffering from grief complications you have no way of really knowing how severe the issue is. That's why seeking the support of others is emphasized in the previous chapter, as they could be the ones who are able to spot any signs of grief complications you might be depicting.

The severest grief complications can be life threatening or fatal, while others can induce long-term physical or psychological damages to your life. These effects can exist in any number of a wide range of examples, such as emotional problems (developed trust issues as a result of your loss) or your guilt making you wish you had died with or in the place of your loved one. Feeling suicidal is a common consequence of grief complications, self-identified in extended cases where you simply feel as if life is just not worth living anymore.

The mentioned symptoms of the explored grief complications so far still fortunately fall into grief complications you can identify yourself. If you notice yourself suffering from these symptoms associated with grief complications, you'll have to take it upon yourself to seek professional help. Go for counseling or kick-start the process by talking to someone and explaining your concerns. Such self-identifiable symptoms of grief complications further extend to invasive or even haunting images and thoughts of your departed loved one, or prolonged instances of still holding on to the hope that your loss wasn't real.

When you start to imagine and truly believe that you haven't experienced any loss (perhaps you believe your loved one is still alive) and you go on with your life as if nothing at all happened, this is when you probably can't diagnose yourself to be suffering from grief complications. This is when your efforts to share your grief with others will pay off and save you from total self-destruction.

The rule of thumb is that you can never get too much help and there is never a reason too small to pass up an opportunity to seek professional psychiatric help. Trained professionals can sometimes put into effect very small treatment solutions which can have a major impact on issues that you'd otherwise not have managed to uncover yourself.

Professional medical or psychiatric help doesn't always have to be administered in a formal manner. You can attend specialized grief-healing retreats, some of which are even available via the likes of day spas or holistic/alternative centers.

Chapter 5: Honoring the Memory of Your Departed Loved One

The best way to cope with your loss and work your way towards healing is honoring the memory of the loved one you've lost. You undoubtedly already know that the aim is NOT to forget about whom or what you lost, but rather to move on with your new life without their physical presence.

Make an effort to honor the memory of your loss by casting your mind back to the good times you had. If it's a loved one you've lost, share good-time memories with other people with whom the loss is shared. Keep some of their belongings for yourself, maintain old traditions you had with them and you can even make new traditions in their memory. Nothing works better in honoring a departed loved one's memory than creating a memorial in their honor, even if by simply committing to doing something of your choosing as a dedication to their memory.

Pretty much the same principles apply to the loss of a pet, but if your grief was caused by something physical or by a set of circumstances you were previously in control of acquiring, as hard as it is, look at it as a challenge to dust yourself off and build an even better life for yourself. Allow yourself to grieve, but get right back up on the horse and learn to ride again.

Conclusion

Grief is the process of dealing with a significant loss, either of a loved one through death, via an ended relationship or even the loss of something like a life-long dream or set of circumstances.

Different people naturally react differently to loss and that's essentially why people should be allowed to grieve differently, in their own unique ways. While you should indeed find your own way of grieving as part of your efforts to cope with your loss and heal, understanding the five stages of grief will go a long way in helping you work out exactly where you are and give you some direction by way of how to move on. These five stages include denial, anger, bargaining, depression and acceptance, experienced in no particular order and with varying degrees of intensity and time durations.

There are various myths surrounding grief, most of which try to dictate to grievers how they should conduct their grieving process. When these myths give way to facts however, you can learn to better cope with the loss of a loved one by firstly taking control of your grieving process and secondly building up a support structure around you.

The process of grieving can sometimes bring about serious complications and you need to know how to deal with them after identifying them through their common symptoms. Left unattended, these complications can account for life-threatening effects or instill permanent health and psychological damages. This is when the constructed support group comes into play to off-set the associated risks, particularly if you as the griever aren't aware of the complications arising out of your grief.

A huge and vital part of coping with grief and healing after the loss of a loved one takes the form of not trying to forget them, but rather honoring their memory through various ways.

Finally, I'd like to thank you for purchasing this book! If you found it helpful, I'd greatly appreciate it if you'd take a moment to leave a review on Amazon. Thank you!

20051413R00026

Printed in Poland
by Amazon Fulfillment
Poland Sp. z o.o., Wrocław